Kindle Fire HD
User's Manual

The Ultimate Guide to Getting Started, Tips, Tricks, Applications and More

Disclaimer

No part of this book can be transmitted or reproduced in any form including print, electronic, photocopying, scanning, mechanical or recording without prior written permission from the author.

While the author has taken utmost efforts to ensure accuracy of the written content, all readers are advised to follow information mentioned herein at their own risk. The author cannot be held responsible for any personal or commercial damage caused by misinterpretation of information or improper use of the device.

All information, ideas and guidelines presented here are for educational purpose only. **This book cannot be used to replace information provided with the device.** All readers are encouraged to seek professional advice when needed.

What Will You Find in this Report?

You absolutely love your new Kindle Fire HD and this book will show you all what can be done with this wonderful gadget. This book is put together with an intention to help all tech enthusiasts get more out of their favorite tablet.

A lot of amazing things can be done with Kindle Fire HD and you can miss out on a lot of things if you don't know about the remarkable features this device offers. This book is perfect for every Kindle Fire HD user. You will get to know the different settings of your gadget including basic settings, Wi-Fi connection, email information and how you can download applications.

As the report will progress, you will also learn ways to add Kindle books, movies, music and other entertainment to your device. You can also find the list of must have apps right here that will help you unleash many exciting and powerful features of your Kindle Fire HD. This book also takes a tour into special tricks and tips that will help you get your Kindle Fire HD running.

In short, this book will give you everything you need to take your gadget to the next level. So, let's get started and explore your Kindle Fire HD to make it more interactive and easy to handle.

Table of Contents

10.Conclusion

1. What is Kindle Fire HD?

Kindle Fire HD is the second generation of Kindle Fire tablets launched by Amazon. The first 7" Kindle Fire HD was released on September 14, 2012. Its 8.9" version was released on November 16, 2012. Presently, the 8.9" model of this amazing gadget is only available in the United States.

Those of you who think that Kindle Fire HD is only useful for downloading and reading eBooks, you should know that this gadget has a lot more to offer. You get a chance to enter the exciting world of music, applications, movies and games through the stunning HD display screen.

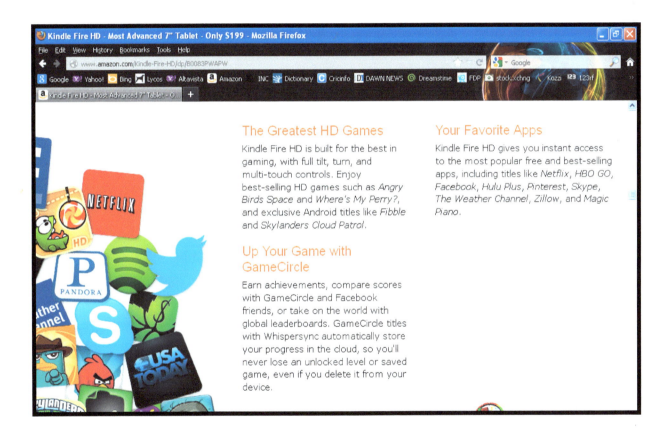

If you are holding Kindle Fire HD in your hands right now, you'll know that its display is bright and rich. The exclusive stereo speakers give you the most awesome sound you've ever heard. Its excellent Wi-Fi connectivity gives you instant access to a wide genre of content.

What's even more amazing about this tablet is the fact that the high resolution display has an anti-glare technology. This not only brings your content to life but you can easily use the gadget even under overhead light.

Since Kindle Fire HD is all about viewing content in high definition, your gadget optimizes sound to make your experience even more interesting. The sound you hear depends on what you are doing at that point in time. Let's say if you are listening to music, the exclusive speakers will convey sound in a different way compared to what you'll hear if you are taking on Skype.

If you have been using tablets, you know that slow video buffering or download speed spoils your web browsing experience. Kindle Fire HD gets rid of this issue as the device has state-of-the-art dual Wi-Fi antenna for faster downloads.

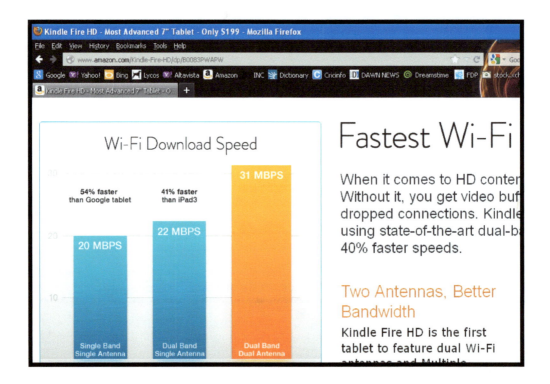

When you have two antennas, there will be fewer dropped connections or slow downloads. In addition to faster download speeds and a rich HD display, Kindle Fire HD delivers excellent performance with over 11 hours of battery life. Your videos play faster, your games proceed smoothly and your home screen is really quick, all because of the powerful HD processor contained in your device.

2.Advantages of Kindle Fire HD

Technical specifications of Kindle Fire HD are really interesting. This exciting tablet weights 395g and with 7 inches dimensions, it can fit inside a purse. It looks good because when compared to original Kindle, the new Kindle Fire HD is taller and thinner.

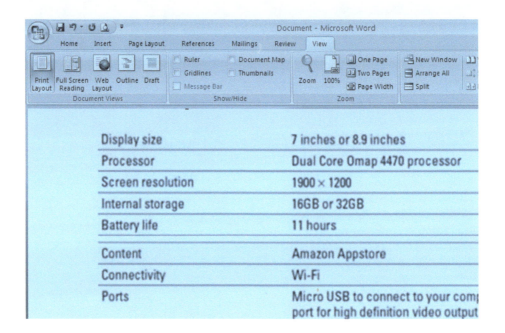

Display size	7 inches or 8.9 inches
Processor	Dual Core Omap 4470 processor
Screen resolution	1900 × 1200
Internal storage	16GB or 32GB
Battery life	11 hours
Content	Amazon Appstore
Connectivity	Wi-Fi
Ports	Micro USB to connect to your comp port for high definition video output

As with any tablet, tech savvy users are keen to know more about the operating system. Kindle Fire HD is based on Android OS launched by Google. This is not enough. Amazon has customized the Android system to give a simpler interface and help you run Kindle Fire HD applications. Since the tablet has a simple interface, it can be used by anyone including users who are not tech savvy.

The enhanced screen display makes movies and videos look real and text becomes easy to read. Amazon claims that your gadget can give 11 hours of uninterrupted video playback when fully charged.

Dual Wi-Fi antenna gives great download speed and you have a chance to install a number of useful applications on your tablet. The feature that really makes Kindle Fire HD so popular is access to Amazon's extensive media library.

You can have lots of music, videos, magazines and eBooks delivered directly to your tablet. Those of who are interested in numbers will be quite pleased to know that there are more than 20 million songs in the music store. You can find more information about importing music and videos to your Kindle Fire HD later in this guide.

Not to forget, Kindle Fire HD is really kind to your ears. The device automatically enhances sound based on the application you are using.

Amazon has not neglected the importance of storage space. You get 16 GB of storage space on the device along with access to Amazon's cloud storage. Kindle Fire HD users suggest that this is the best tablet deal in terms of storage.

3.Getting Started with the Device

i.   Turning Kindle Fire HD On and Off

Once Kindle Fire HD gets out of its original packaging, it is time to turn it on. Remove the plastic sleeve that comes with the tablet and hold the device in portrait mode.

You can find the power button on the right side of the Kindle. Along with the power button, you can also find a headphone jack and the right speaker.

To turn the device on, press the power button. Your home screen will then show up after 10 to 15 seconds. Place your finger on the lock icon that appears on the screen to unlock your device. You can then start using and enjoying your Kindle Fire HD.

If you want to lock your tablet or put it to 'sleep', gently tap the power button. Make sure you release the power button quickly.

To switch off the device, hold the power button until you see a message on the screen. You will find two options offering you to shut down the tablet or cancel your request.

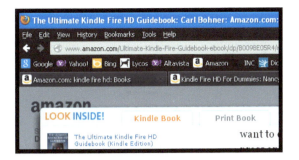

Tap shut down option to power off your device or hit the cancel option if you wish to change your decision.

Friendly Reminders:

a) If your Kindle Fire HD becomes unresponsive at any point, gently hold and press the power button for 15 to 20 seconds. The device will be turned off. Restart your Kindle again by pressing the power button. This should bring it back to life.

b) Don't be surprised if your Kindle goes to sleep when it hits a hard surface. Maybe the power button was oriented at the bottom and you accidently hit it while showing something to your friend.

ii.   Charging the Battery

Kindle Fire HD is supplied with a USB cable which can be used for charging. Your device is not fully charged when you receive it. All you have to do is connect your tablet to a computer via the USB cable. In case you don't want to charge Kindle Fire HD by connecting to your computer, you can use the same USB cable to connect your device to a power adapter (sold separately).

Here, you have to use a charging device (which is not included with your product). You can find more information about useful accessories under section xiv. Kindle Fire HD users have one common question.

"How Do I Know My Kindle Fire HD Is Charging or Not?"

Once you connect your Kindle Fire HD to a power adapter or your computer, light next to the power button will appear yellow. This shows that your device is connected properly and is charging. The light changes to green when your tablet is fully charged.

Here is a table to give you an idea about the estimated charging time using different options.

Charging Option Used with USB Cable	Estimated Charging Time For Battery (From 0% to 100%)
Kindle PowerFast Charger	3.7 hrs
White Kindle Power Adapter (5W)	4.4 hrs
Standard PC USB Port	10.4 hrs

Friendly Reminders:

a) If you are charging your tablet using the computer, connect the USB cable directly to a USB port on your computer.

b) It is better if your computer remains plugged into a power supply when your Kindle Fire HD is charging. Sometimes your computer may not have sufficient power to charge the tablet if it is not plugged in.

c) Make sure your computer stays active when your tablet is charging. You can disable sleep, hibernate or standby modes if required.

d) In case your Kindle does not recognize the USB connection, unplug the cable and reconnect your device. If the problem persists, you need to change the USB port you are currently using.

e) If you use a Kindle micro USB cable (sold separately) to charge your tablet from a computer, charging time will be reduced to four to six hours.

f) You'll see a tiny lightning bolt on the battery icon on your home screen. This indicates that your Kindle Fire HD is still charging.

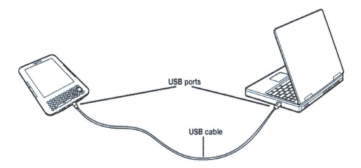

g) If you want to optimize battery life of your Kindle Fire HD, you can try the following tips.

    A. Lower the brightness of your display.

    B. Turn off Bluetooth and Wi-Fi.

    C. Use headphones instead of speakers.

D. Change ***Inbox Check*** frequency for your email accounts.

E. Charge the battery in a temperature range from 32 to 95 degrees Fahrenheit (i.e. 0 to 35 degrees Celsius).

iii. Interacting with the Touch-Screen

Locking and Unlocking Your Screen

Swipe the lock icon as shown in the figure below to unlock your Kindle Fire HD. Once the device is unlocked, you can swipe the finger to scroll up or down within your home screen or view menu. You can tap on the screen to select text and numbers using the onscreen keyboard.

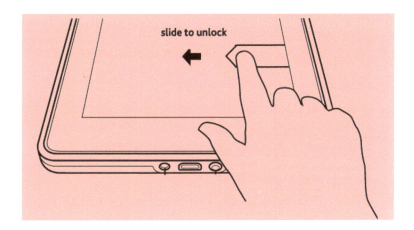

Lock screen also appears when you wake your tablet from sleep mode or switch it on. To unlock the screen, simply swipe your finger from the right side to left.

Setting Up Lock Screen Passwords

If you want to restrict access of your tablet, you can set a lock screen password.

1. Unlock the screen and swipe downwards from the top. Tap **More** from the menu bar.

2. Tap Security and move to **Lock Screen Password**.

3. Tap **On** and enter a password you wish to use. Make sure your password is numeric and contains at least four characters.

4. Once done, tap **Finish**.

You have to enter the same numeric password the next time you want to unlock your screen. In case you forget your password, you have to reset your tablet to default factory settings to gain access. However, you'll also have to download all contents again.

Screen Rotation

Sometimes your Kindle Fire HD screen will rotate when you are trying to read a book or want to watch a movie. This can become really annoying especially if it happens quite often. But, you can get rid of it easily. All you have to do is disable screen rotation and 'fix' your display.

There are two options when you talk about screen rotation. You can either lock or unlock screen rotation. Swipe your finger downwards and enter the setting menu.

When you see the following toolbar, tap the icon highlighted in the figure below to lock or unlock screen rotation. When the icon says '**Locked**', screen rotation is disabled. However, if you tap the icon again, it displays '**Unlocked**' and screen rotation is enabled for your tablet.

Screen rotation is disabled

Screen will rotate when you change the position of your tablet

Screen Savers

When you choose to buy a Kindle Fire HD, you get it with sponsored screensavers and special offers. Since your tablet comes with bonus offers, you can get

1. Movie posters

2. Book covers

3. Music covers

4. Special deals on digital content

5. Special deals on electronics directly on your home screen.

The offers will be displayed in the lower left hand corner of your home screen; however, this will not interrupt your use of the tablet. If you decide to change your mind and want to opt out of the sponsored screensavers and special offers, you can do so after making a payment.

Method to Unsubscribe Sponsored Screensavers and Other Special Offers

1. Visit www.amazon.com/manageyourkindle and go to your Kindle Account.

2. Click Manage Your Devices and go to Special Offers.

3. Click Edit (appears next to Subscribed) and tap Unsubscribe Now. You will see a window with instructions to unsubscribe your offer.

How Do I Set My Kindle Fire HD to Have Screensaver or Wallpapers?

Many of you want to know whether or not there is a way to change wallpapers on your Kindle Fire HD. Presently, you can change the wallpaper easily by downloading an application called **"My Kindle Wallpaper"**

This is the valuable application that allows you to change the wallpaper without the need of rooting your device. Details about rooting your device can be found later in this guide. **"My Kindle Wallpaper"** gives you two options to set wallpapers. You can choose the Single Image mode or opt for Wallpaper Folder mode.

Single Image mode is similar to what you do on your laptop or computer. You can select an image and the application will set it as your Kindle Fire HD wallpaper.

Wallpaper Folder mode changes your wallpaper every time your tablet screen is turned on.

How You Can Install "My Kindle Wallpaper"

To download this application, you need to first allow your tablet to install applications from an unknown source. If you want to know how you can do this, don't forget to check out the section on *Installing Applications on Your Device* under chapter 5.

After you allow Kindle Fire HD to install applications, you can download the application directly to your tablet. You will see file progress in the notification bar. Once download is completed, click the file notification icon.

You will then be directed to a permission page. These permissions are mostly related to system tools. You can allow the application to set wallpapers and start running when the device is turned on.

Once you are done with permissions, Click **Install**. After installation is complete, click **Open** to start using your application. You will see a setting screen first. Click **Enable My Kindle Wallpaper**. If you want to stop using this application at anytime, you can **disable My Kindle Wallpaper**.

Once you disable My Kindle Wallpaper, your tablet wallpaper will be restored to default system wallpaper. After you enable the application, you can select the wallpaper mode.

If you select **Single Image** mode, the application will display your image gallery. Choose the image that you want to see as your wallpaper. You also have the option to crop the image or modify the image area.

If you choose **Wallpaper Folder** mode, My Kindle Wallpaper allows you to browse to your images folder and then select an image. As mentioned earlier, the wallpaper will change every time you turn your screen on.

iv.   Basic Settings

What are the main settings of your Kindle Fire HD?

Your Kindle Fire HD has the following hardware controls.

Microphone

Headphone jack

Display Screen (7" or 8.9" HD)

Front Facing Camera

Dolby audio stereo speakers

Power and volume adjustment button

Ports for connecting headphones, microUSB and micro-HDMI

Let's now take a look at Kindle Fire HD menus. If you have upgraded from an older version of Kindle Fire to Kindle Fire HD, you'll find the menu to be very familiar. The controls and options are the same; however, there are some greatly improved performance features.

Even if you are new to Kindle Fire HD, you will still find this device really easy to use. Here is a brief description to make you more familiar with your new gadget.

Every time you turn on your tablet, you will find a **Status Bar**. This bar is located right at the top of your HD screen. The status bar displays notifications, battery icon, Wi-Fi indicator and the Bluetooth indicator. You will also find a Location Based Services indicator.

❷ **Notifications**

Notifications basically, are messages generated by games and applications installed on your device. You can select a sound to inform you about the incoming notifications from the settings menu.

 Wi-Fi Indicator

This indicator is very useful to know the strength of Wi-Fi signals at your location. The number of bands you see on the status bar tell you whether or not you have strong signals in your area.

Bluetooth

The Bluetooth icon will appear in the status bar whenever Bluetooth is turned on. It will also turn blue when you pair or connect your Kindle Fire HD to another Bluetooth device.

Location-Based Services

The icon (compass) appears when you use a location based application. However, the icon appears only when you enable Location-Based Services under the settings menu. Your Kindle Fire HD uses Wi-Fi to guess your location.

Battery Indicator

This icon shows the amount of battery charge remaining in Kindle Fire HD. Make sure you charge your tablet when battery charge gets low.

v. Notifications

Here is some information to help you understand Kindle Fire HD notifications. Most first-time Kindle Fire HD users are confused when it comes to setting notifications for their tablet. They have one common question:

How do I set up my Kindle Fire HD's notifications?

You can access notifications by swiping down from the top of your Kindle fire HD screen. When you 'pull' the screen down, you will see notifications generated by the applications installed on your tablet. Tap the notification to view details and tap **Clear All** to remove all notifications.

Notifications you'll receive also include system alerts and progress of file download. Sometimes applications and games can get really annoying and generate notifications for no reason. The good news is that you can now set notifications for individual applications installed on your tablet.

First swipe down from the top of your screen. You will see the following menu bar.

To proceed, go to **More**, then settings menu and tap applications. Make sure you turn on or turn off notifications as desired. You also need to remember that some applications have notifications turned off by default. To make sure that you don't miss out on something important, check your Kindle Fire settings. Notifications for application need to be turned on if you want to see them on your screen.

vi.   Volume

How Can You Turn the Volume Up/Down on Your Kindle Fire HD?

It is really easy to adjust volume on Kindle Fire HD. Unlock your device and swipe down from the top of the screen. Tap the volume icon (highlighted above) to adjust the volume.

You can also increase or decrease the volume of your Kindle Fire HD using the volume buttons on the outside edge. You can find them right next to the power button.

The volume buttons on Kindle Fire HD are an improvement over older versions of Kindle Fire. Additional volume settings are available when you are playing a game or want to listen to your favorite soundtrack. This option is also accessible when you watch a video on your Kindle Fire HD.

vii.   Display

If you swipe your screen down, a brightness icon will appear in the quick settings bar. Tap the icon and adjust the slider to change the brightness of your screen. Tap **More** to access other display settings.

When you tap display under 'More', you have the option to adjust screen brightness as well as specify the amount of time your Kindle Fire HD can be inactive before going to sleep.

viii.   Fonts and Other Related Items

You cannot change the font or text size of menus or home screen in Kindle Fire HD. However, you do have the option of changing font size and type when you are reading an eBook.

To do this, tap the settings button in the reading toolbar. You can view and customize settings for font size, type, page margins and color mode.

ix.   Using the Camera

The front facing camera allows you to make video calls and chat with friends using Skype. Your Kindle Fire HD has a built-in camera that faces the person who is holding the device.

Skype is a useful application that helps you make free video calls and free voice calls to family and friends around the globe. You can also use Skype to send instant messages to other contacts.

How Can You Take Pictures And Shoot Videos Using Kindle Fire HD?

As mentioned earlier, Kindle Fire HD has a front facing camera that can be used for video chat. If you've been looking for ways to take a few snapshots, you need to know that the process is a little different compared to a regular tablet or smartphone. Here are a few tips to help you take cool pictures using your tablet.

If you want to capture a screenshot, you have to press and hold the volume down and the power button at the same time. Yes, it may take some time before you get really perfect, but this trick will work. The screenshots will be placed in the photo section. Your folder will be named screenshots.

Video Recording and Taking Panoramic Photos

You have to open the camera application on your Kindle Fire HD to access the 'full camera' features.

1. Install ES File Explorer from Amazon.com. You can find this application under "Apps for Android".
2. After successful installation, open ES File Explorer and tap the icon that appears in the upper right corner. This icon is also known as "AppMgr".

3. Tap the Category icon and then select "System Apps".

4. Hit the Camera icon and tap open.

That's it. You can use the camera to take photos and record videos. Currently, there is no way you can add 'camera' to your home screen. So, you have to access the camera using ES File Explorer.

Download ***PicShop Lite Photo Editor*** from Amazon .com to edit and customize your photos and screenshots.

x.   Parental Control

Setting parental control on your device allows you to decide applications, books, videos and content that can be accessed by kids. You can restrict access to applications and other content by setting up passwords.

Parental Controls on Kindle Fire HD can be applied to:

1. Web browsing

2. Shopping from the Amazon Store

3. Your email, calendar and contacts applications

4. Amazon Instant Video and Prime Instant Video

5. Specific content including eBooks and games

6. Wireless connectivity

How Can You Set Parental Control Password to Restrict Access?

1. Parental control can be accessed after swiping down from the top of the screen. Tap **More > Parental Control** to customize access.

2. Tap **Parental Controls On**.

3. Kindle Fire HD will ask you to enter a password. Enter your desired password, confirm your entry and then select finish.

4. After you have set a password, you can select items you want to restrict.

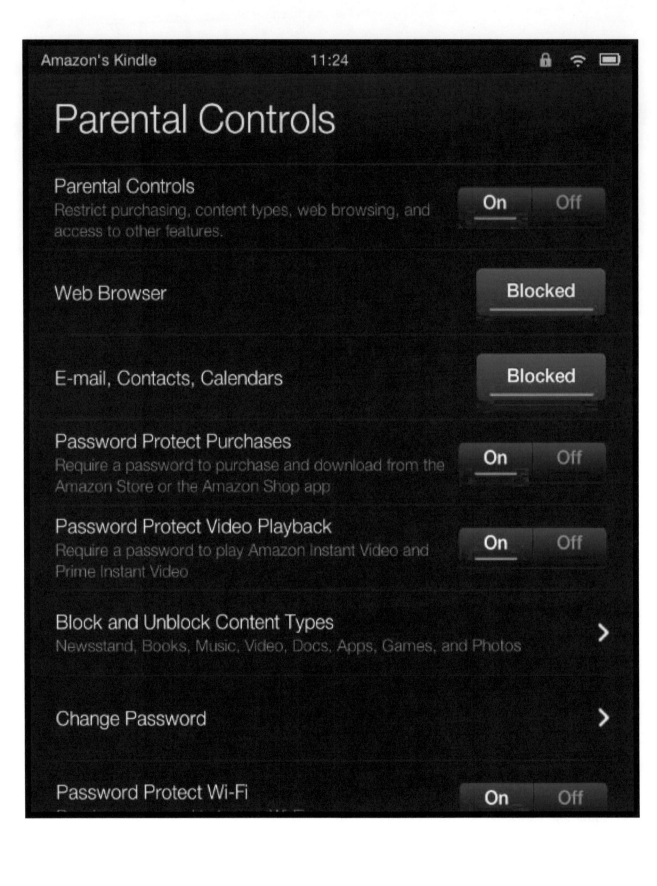

Parental Controls

Parental Controls
Restrict purchasing, content types, web browsing, and access to other features.

On   Off

Web Browser

Blocked

E-mail, Contacts, Calendars

Blocked

Password Protect Purchases
Require a password to purchase and download from the Amazon Store or the Amazon Shop app

On   Off

Password Protect Video Playback
Require a password to play Amazon Instant Video and Prime Instant Video

On   Off

Block and Unblock Content Types
Newsstand, Books, Music, Video, Docs, Apps, Games, and Photos

>

Change Password

>

Password Protect Wi-Fi

On   Off

What If I Want to Change Parental Controls Settings or Password?

1. Swipe your finger down from the top of your screen.

2. Tap **More > Parental Controls.**

3. Enter your password and tap **Change Password.**

4. You can also change parental control settings for different content.

Note:

In case you forget your password, you will have to restore your Kindle Fire HD to original factory settings to change parental control. Remember, restoring factory settings means that you have to register your tablet again and re-download all content.

How Can You Reset Your Kindle Fire HD To Factory Settings?

This is really simple.

1. Unlock your screen and swipe down.

2. Tap **More**, and then hit **"Device".**

3. Tap **Reset to Factory Defaults** to restore your tablet to original settings.

Kindle FreeTime

Kindle FreeTime is an exciting application included on Kindle Fire HD that allows you to create a unique viewing experience for kids. Kids then can only access content featured in their respective Kindle FreeTime profile.

Advantages for Parents

1. Choose games, applications, videos and books kids can view.

2. Create customized profiles for up to six children.

3. Establish limits to Kindle Fire HD use.

4. Prevent access to content outside Kindle FreeTime profile.

Interestingly, Kindle FreeTime application blocks access to the web browser, Amazon shopping store, social networking websites (such as Facebook and Twitter) and location based services.

Why Kids Love Kindle FreeTime?

1. Content can be viewed in a kid-friendly interface.

2. Kids can add items to their list of favorites. Favorites can then be viewed by tapping the "star" showing up on the home screen.

3. Kids can navigate content based on their visual appearance.

xi.   Keyboard

Kindle Fire HD has an onscreen keyboard which you can use to enter text and numbers. Whenever you have to enter text such during internet browsing, the onscreen keyboard will appear. Your keyboard will be something like this.

You can tap ?123 to switch the keyboard view to numbers and symbols.

Tap ABC again to switch back to default keyboard i.e. alphabet display.

The arrow or ⇧ can be used as a shift key for upper case letters. If you want to lock your keyboard and use uppercase letters, tap the arrow twice.

Similar to your regular keyboard, you can clear your entry using the Delete tab.

xii.   Cleaning the Screen

Your Kindle Fire HD screen can get greasy as you use your fingers to 'push and pull the content'. If you need to clean your screen, use the same soft cloth you normally use to clean your glasses.

Remember, you should avoid using harsh chemicals and rough fabrics on your screen. Take care not to touch your screen excessively. And if you need to touch your screen quite often, use a soft cotton cloth to gently wipe off the dust and stains.

In case you find a liquid stain on your screen, wipe it carefully using a slightly damp cloth. You can also buy a screen protector and a sturdy cover for your Kindle Fire HD so that your screen remains safe even if you place your tablet in your briefcase, purse or back pack.

xiii.   Change Your Kindle Fire HD Name

To change the name that appears in the upper left corner of your Kindle Fire HD, you need to first login to your account on Amazon. Enter your email id and secure password and then go to **Manage Your Devices** page. You can then edit the name and change it to whatever you desire.

xiv.   Some Useful Accessories for Your Device

1. Amazon Kindle PowerFast

This powerful adapter will fully charge your Kindle Fire HD 7" in less than four hours. Since the power adapter is optimized for Kindle Fire and Kindle Fire HD tablets, you can use it with the black USB cable included with your new device. Amazon Kindle PowerFast's prongs can be folded conveniently so you can take the adapter along with you when you travel.

2. Standing Leather Case for Kindle Fire HD 7"

Available in different colors, this standing leather case can be used as a built in stand. You can enjoy hands free viewing experience as the thin case secures your 7" Kindle Fire HD. Moreover, you can open or close the case to wake or put your tablet to sleep.

3. Marware 3-Pack Ultra-Clear Screen Protector

Optimized for quick and easy installation, Marware 3-Pack Ultra-Clear Screen Protector can be used on 7" Kindle Fire HD screen. You also receive a microfiber cleaning cloth along with an applicator card when you buy this product.

Installing screen protector on your device keeps your tablet clear of smudges, stains and finger prints.

You can browse more accessories by visiting http://www.amazon.com/Kindle-Accessories/b/ref=sv_kstore_6?ie=UTF8&node=1268192011.

Amazon.com: Marware 3-Pack Ultra-Clear Screen Protector for Kindle Fire HD 7" (will only fit Kindle Fire HD 7"): Kindle Store - Mozilla Firefox

File   Edit   View   History   Bookmarks   Tools   Help

www.amazon.com/Marware-3-Pack-Ultra-Clear-Screen-Protector/dp/B00902S3Y8/ref=sr_1_2?s=fiona-hardware&ie=UTF8&qid=1:   Google

Google   Yahoo!   Bing   Lycos   Altavista   Amazon   INC   Dictionary   Cricinfo   DAWN NEWS   Dreamstime   FDP   stock.xchng   Kozzi   123   123rf

40 Tips and Tricks for Kindle Fire HD (Vide...   Amazon.com: Marware 3-Pack Ultra-Clea...   X   +

amazon
Join Prime

Your Amazon.com   Today's Deals   Gift Cards   Help

Top Holiday Deals
New deals every day

> Shop now
Presented by T-Mob

Shop by
Department   Search   Kindle Store ▼   Go   Hello. Sign in
Your Account   Join
Prime▼   0 Cart▼   Wish
List ▼

Kindle Store   Buy A Kindle   Free Reading Apps   Kindle eBooks   Kindle Singles   Newsstand   Popular Games   Accessories   Discussions

Marware 3-Pack Ultra-Clear Screen Protector for Kindle Fire HD 7" (will only fit Kindle Fire HD 7")

by Marware

★★★½☆ ☑ (159 customer reviews) | 👍 Like (36)

List Price: $19.99

Price: $14.99 & eligible for FREE Super Saver Shipping on orders over $25. Details

You Save: $5.00 (25%)

Special Offers Available

In Stock.
Ships from and sold by **Amazon.com**.

Quantity: 1 ▼

☐
Yes, I want **FREE Two-Day Shipping** with Amazon Prime

Add to Cart

or

Sign in to turn on 1-Click ordering.

Add to Wish List

More Buying Choices

xv. Troubleshooting

Problems with Kindle Fire HD Battery

1. If your battery isn't charging, make sure you have connected your device properly. Always use power adapters and USB cables optimized for Kindle Fire HD to charge your tablet. It can take up to 4 hours or longer to fully charge your tablet if the battery has been fully consumed.

2. If your Kindle Fire HD is not holding charge, turn off the Wi-Fi when you are reading books or want to watch videos. Activities such as web browsing and file download consume more battery and deplete battery charge really quickly.

Problems with Kindle Fire HD Passwords

You only have four attempts to enter your valid password. If you forget your password or enter a wrong password more than four times, you have to restore your tablet to factory settings. This will clear your downloaded items and you also have to register your device again.

Problems with USB Connection

1. If your computer does not recognize your device, unplug the device and try connecting it again. You can also try a different USB port or USB cable if the problem persists.

2. Mac users have to install an Android File Transfer application to transfer files to Kindle Fire HD via USB.

If Your Kindle Fire HD Gets Stolen

Never leave your device unattended at public places. If your tablet gets stolen, deregister your device by going to Manage Your Kindle page. Don't forget to cancel all your active subscriptions through the same page. You can contact your local police if you want to file a police complaint.

Kindle Fire HD and International Travelers

If you want to travel with your Kindle Fire HD, you can access any content downloaded on your device. You can purchase new content for your device even you are outside the United States with a U.S. credit card, however there are certain restrictions.

You have to be present in the United States to purchase or download TV shows and stream movies. All downloads and purchases related to stream movies and TV shows require you to submit a valid U.S. billing address. Currently, music purchases from Amazon.com are only available to customers present in the U.S. If you have plans to travel abroad, you can download this content for later use prior to leaving United States.

Pairing Devices on Bluetooth

Turn on the device you want to pair with Kindle Fire HD. Then, go to **Settings > Wireless > Bluetooth** on your tablet. Enable Bluetooth and tap your tablet's name to make it visible.

Kindle Fire HD normally scans and shows Bluetooth devices in the range. If the device you want to connect does not show up automatically, hit "search for devices" on your tablet. You can then connect the two devices.

4.The Next Steps

i.   Registering the Device

You have to register your device before you can start using all of the features. In order to register, you have to first connect to a Wi-Fi network. How you can connect to a wireless network is discussed in the next section.

Once you register your device, you can search and shop for applications, books, videos, music and movies.

Process for Registering Your Device

1. Enter your valid email address and password at Amazon.com. You will login to your Amazon account. (You can refer to onscreen keyboard to know how you can enter alphabets and numbers)

2. Tap the **Register** button and your device will be registered successfully.

3. If you don't have an Amazon account, go to create account on Amazon.com.

4. Follow the instructions to create a new account and complete the registration process.

5. If the page displays "Deregister" instead of "Register", this means your tablet is already registered on a different Amazon account. First **Deregister your tablet** and then register it to your personal Amazon account.

6. Once you've completed the registration process, you can select your time zone and confirm your personal account.

ii.   Setting Up Kindle Fire HD Wi-Fi

Can You Connect to the Internet Everywhere?

The good news is that your Kindle Fire HD automatically detects Wi-Fi networks that are available in your area. You can connect to the internet in every area that has Wi-Fi access.

How You Can Connect to Wi-Fi:

1. As mentioned earlier, your tablet automatically detects Wi-Fi networks within reach. Tap the name of the network you want to connect to.

2. You will then connect to the network successfully. Enter network password if required. In case you don't know the network password, you have to contact the person who manages your network.

3. Your Kindle Fire HD will automatically connect to the same Wi-Fi network the same time it detects the same signals.

How Can You turn on and Turn off the Kindle Fire HD Wi-Fi?

This process is really simple. To turn on the Kindle Fire HD Wi-Fi, swipe down from the top of your screen and hit **Wireless**. Make sure Airplane Mode is turned off on your device.

You will find a list of Wi-Fi networks that are available on your screen; however, this may take some time. Tap the network you want to connect and enter password if required.

To turn off the Wi-Fi, swipe down from the top of your screen again and tap "Off".

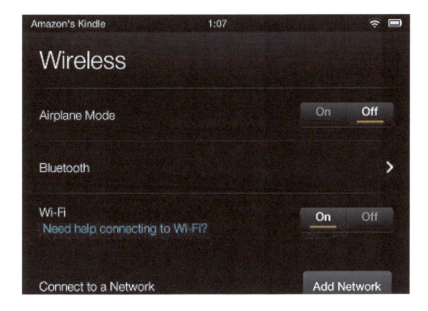

If Kindle Fire HD does not detect the Wi-Fi network, you need to add it manually.

1. You need to know the network name and password before you can connect manually.

2. Make sure you are within the working range of the desired network.

3. Unlock your device and swipe down from the top of the screen. Make sure that Airplane Mode is turned **Off**.

4. Enable Wi-Fi connection and then tap **Add Network**.

5. Enter the name (i.e. Network SSID) of the Wi-Fi network you want to connect to.

6. Choose encryption mode under **Security** menu. You have to enter a password if you enter encryption mode other than open.

7. Tap **Save**, and then **Connect**. Your password will be saved and Kindle Fire HD will be connected to the new network.

I Want My Kindle Fire HD to Forget a Wi-Fi Network

Your Kindle Fire HD will automatically connect to a Wi-Fi network featured under Wireless when it detects signals from the same network. However, if you don't want it to happen in the future, you can "forget" the network.

To forget a network, tap **Wireless** after swiping down from the top of your screen. Tap the name of the network and hit **Forget** to remove it from your list.

iii.   What You Can Store on Your Device

Remember, your Kindle Fire can store books, movies, videos, music, applications and more. However, your tablet will only recognize and play files that are supported by the device. The content you store on your tablet also needs to be free of digital rights management (DRM) software.

Here is a list of file types supported by your Kindle Fire HD.

Document Formats: TXT, DOCX, DOC, PDF, MOBI, PRC and AZW.

Audio Formats (Music): MP3, WAV, MIDI, OGG and Non-DRM AAC (.m4a).

Images Formats: JPEG, PNG, BMP and GIF.

Video Formats: MP4 only.

---

iv.   Cloud and Device Storage Options

Kindle Fire HD is available with an internal storage capacity of 16 or 32 GB. In addition to device storage, you get unlimited storage space on the Amazon cloud. You can use cloud storage for content downloaded from the Amazon Store.

v.   Get Extra Storage and Memory

How can I add more storage to my Kindle Fire HD?

Presently, you can add cloud storage options to save your important files and documents. Cloud options that work really well with Kindle Fire HD include SugarSync and Dropbox. SugarSync can be downloaded from the Amazon application store, while Dropbox can be downloaded from https://www.dropbox.com/android

vi.   Using the Carousel

The Carousel shows up on your home screen and displays content that you view recently. It will feature books, videos, applications, music and magazines you have accessed not long time back.

Browsing through the carousel is really easy. Move your fingers across the screen to browse through the selection and view all items. If you want to select an item, all you have to do is tap it. Remember, items in the carousel are displayed with most recent ones first. If you have purchased any music or video from the Amazon store, it will be shown as **New**.

There is some good news for all you reading fans. Bookmark badges in the carousel show how much of the book you have read.

Music Library

Playing Music on Kindle Fire HD

Music stored on your device can be accessed and enjoyed anytime without a Wi-Fi connection. You can also play and download music you buy from Amazon.com without any restriction. If you want to download your favorite soundtrack from the Cloud player to your tablet, press the song, artist collection or playlist for a little while and then tap **Download**. The track will be saved in your device library that can be accessed even when you don't have an internet connection.

Loading Music from USB

How Can You Transfer Music From Your PC To Kindle Fire?

Music, videos, books, photos and documents from your computer (Windows or Mac) can be transferred to your Kindle Fire HD. This is possible using the USB cable that is provided with your tablet. One thing you need to keep in mind is that content transferred from your computer will be stored in your device, not the cloud storage.

Before you transfer the files, you need to first connect your tablet to your computer using the USB cable. Make sure your tablet is switched on and unlocked before you connect the cable. Once you plug in your device into your Windows or Mac computer, it will appear as a removable storage device.

For Windows computer users, Kindle Fire HD appears as a removable storage device or external device under **My Computer or Computer**. Mac users can spot Kindle Fire HD on their desktop.

1. Enter Kindle Fire HD drive and then double click **Internal Storage.**

2. Locate and select music files you want to transfer on your computer.

3. Drag and drop the selected files into the relevant folder inside **Internal Storage in Kindle Fire HD drive.** For example, music files should be stored in Music folder and images should be dropped in Pictures folder.

4. After you finish transferring the files, you can safely eject the device from your computer.

Buying Music

Buying music from the wide selection available at Amazon MP3 store gets really easy when you have a valid **1-Click payment setting** with your Amazon account. You can search and browse tracks by tapping Music on your home screen. Tap **Store** to browse new releases, promotions and MP3 deals. To search for your favorite artist, track or album, tap the search bar that appears on the front.

After you've found your favorite song or album, tap the price button and then select **Buy** or **Get**. Your purchase will be completed using 1-Click payment method. The music you buy from the MP3 store will be stored in Amazon Cloud Player. You can either **Go to your library** to stream or download the soundtracks, or tap **Continue Shopping** to search and purchase more tracks.

You can access **Amazon Cloud Player** by tapping **Music** from your home screen. If you want to remove an album or song you've downloaded on your Kindle Fire HD, just press the song title. Select **Remove Album/Song from device** and tap **Yes** to confirm deletion. The song or album will then be deleted and this will free valuable storage space on your device.

Video Library

How You Can Watch Movies

Amazon Instant Video and Prime Instant Video on Kindle Fire HD give you a chance to watch your favorite movies and TV shows. You can browse and shop for exciting videos by tapping **Video** from your home screen. This video application gives instant access to more than 100,000 movies and TV episodes. The video content is available for rent and purchase.

If you want to stream, buy and download videos to your device, you need to have a Wi-Fi connection. This connection must also be registered to your valid Amazon.com account. If you or any one in your family has an Amazon Prime membership, you can use it to browse and stream hundreds of movies and TV shows from **Prime Instant Video** without paying any extra amount. You can also make purchases from the Amazon store and the videos will be charged by the 1-Click payment method. Remember, you need to have a valid U.S. shipping address to stream and download videos.

How Can You Buy Video

If you find an interesting video and want to purchase it, tap the price button. You will then be shown two options, **Buy** or **Rent**. You can tap the desired option to proceed. If you decide to make a purchase, you will be charged using 1-Click payment method. You can also watch videos while connected to a Wi-Fi network. Tap **Watch Now** to view videos online. You can tap **Download** to save your favorite video on your Kindle Fire HD. The videos you download can be viewed anytime, even without a Wi-Fi connection.

Watching YouTube Videos on Kindle Fire HD

You can access YouTube videos with the help of Silk web browser provided with Kindle Fire HD. However, for a better viewing experience, it is recommended that you download YouTube app for Android from Amazon Appstore.

How You Can Download YouTube Videos to Your Device

Freedi YouTube Downloader is an interesting application you can use to download YouTube videos to your Kindle Fire HD. Sometimes you really want to save the videos you flip through on YouTube. Freedi actually converts YouTube videos into MP4 files which can be directly saved on your device. You can then play the videos even without a Wi-Fi connection. This is a great option if you want to view your favorite YouTube videos later.

Recommendations

When you are using your Kindle Fire HD, you will see **Recommendations** or **Customers Also Bought** beneath the carousel. These recommendations are generated by Amazon.com and you can tap the recommendation to view its details.

Recommendations are related to the products and content you view and buy from the Amazon store. Even though recommendations appear by default, you do have the option of turning them off.

If you don't want to receive further recommendations from Amazon.com, swipe down from the top of your screen and tap **More**. Go to **Applications** and tap **Amazon Home Recommendations.** Tap **Hide** to stop receiving recommendations on your home screen.

Accessing Your Favorites

If you want to add an item in the Carousel to your list of **Favorites**, tap and hold it for sometime. Tap **Add to Favorites** using the message that appears on the screen. You can access your favorites anytime by tapping the tiny star icon that appears at the bottom right corner of your home screen. You can also easily remove items from your Favorites list. All you have to do is tap the star, and then tap and hold the desired item. Tap **Remove from Favorites** using the message that appears on the screen.

How to Sync Your Kindle Fire HD

Your Kindle Fire HD can be synced to your account on Twitter and Facebook. You have the option to sync your social media accounts when you first set up your device. However, you can also do it at any other time you desire. Once you sync your tablet to your accounts, you can share photos, reading highlights, game info and loads of other stuff with ease.

How You Can Connect Kindle Fire HD to Your Facebook or Twitter Account

1. Unlock your device and swipe down from the top of the screen.

2. Tap **More,** and then go to **My Account**.

3. Tap **Manage Social Network Accounts** and choose the accounts you want to sync with your device.

4. Follow the instructions that appear on the screen to complete the process.

5. To remove your account(s), you can return to **Manage Social Networks Account** and tap **Unlink** next to the account you want to remove.

5.Searching for Content

i.   Installing Applications on Your Device

How do I install third party software on Kindle Fire HD?

You can download exciting applications from the Amazon Appstore directly on your Kindle Fire HD. However, if you want to install **3rd Party Apps** or applications from outside, you need to first enable **3rd Party Apps** installation on your device. For this, swipe down from the top of your screen and enter **Settings**. Tap **Device >"Allow Installation of Applications from Unknown sources"** to download third party software.

How do I download apps on Kindle Fire HD?

Downloading and Installing Apps from Amazon Appstore for Android

You can browse and download apps and games to your Kindle Fire HD from Amazon Appstore. Your download and installation will begin automatically when your device is connected to a Wi-Fi network.

If automatic updates are enabled on your device, Amazon Appstore will install latest versions of your downloaded apps with no action needed from your side. You'll find a notification showing that a newer version of an application is successfully installed. If you disable automatic updates, you have to grant permission before installing the updates.

Note:

1. The option for automatic updates for apps downloaded from Amazon store is turned on by default. You can disable updates by going to **Menu > Settings > Automatic updates** and unchecking the box next to **Enable Automatic Updates.**

2. You need to be careful when downloading apps from a third party source. Downloading from unauthorized sites puts your device at an increased risk of malware attack.

ii.   Buying Music and Videos

You can browse and shop for music, videos, books, movies, apps, games and more from Amazon Appstore once you set up your 1-Click Payment Method. You can shop for items by tapping **Shop** on the home screen. If you need to search for items, use the Search box on your screen. You can also refine your search by selecting Departments and other options featured on the side of your screen.

iii. Buying Kindle Books

You can buy Kindle eBooks by visiting Kindle Store on Amazon.com. To purchase eBooks, tap "Store" on your screen. Swipe your finger from right to left to scroll recommendations. You can also browse for titles or best sellers and even review free book samples before making a purchase.

Once you decide to make a purchase, you can click "Buy now" to deliver the eBook to your device. If you want to make purchase later, you can add the item to your wish list and continue shopping.

iv.   What are the MUST HAVE APPS for your Kindle Fire HD?

With so applications to choose from, this list is focused on some of the most popular apps that'll help you enjoy your Kindle Fire HD.

1. Pandora: You can stream radio stations of your choice and personalize your likes and dislikes.

2. HBO Go: This is a must have app if you want to stream your favorite TV show on your tablet.

3. IMDb: If you are a movie fan, you cannot miss out this application. Get the best selection of trailers, movie reviews, behind the scenes and cast details on Kindle Fire HD with IMDb.

4. ESPN ScoreCenter: Staying tuned with the latest sport happening was never this easy. You can keep up with your favorite sport teams and scores with this free application from Amazon.

5. GoodReads: Reading fans need to have this application on Kindle Fire HD. You can even see what your friends are reading when you have GoodReads on your device.

You can browse dozens of other applications on Amazon Appstore and install them on your device.

v. Want to Delete an Application?

Downloaded apps can be removed from your device whenever you want. All you have to do is long press an application in the Device Library and then select **Remove from Device**. Apps you remove from your tablet are stored in the cloud and can be downloaded again. However, if you delete an application permanently, you'll have to purchase the app again before you can re-install it.

vi.   Finding Free Applications and Books

The search feature on the Amazon Appstore page helps you browse through the selection of free applications. A number of suggestions or recommendations will also appear beneath it to help you make a better choice. You can tap on the product or application icon to know more about it.

vii. Downloading Applications, Games, Music and Videos from Your PC

Please refer to "**How Can You Transfer Music From Your PC To Kindle Fire?**" on page 39

to know how you can download content to your Kindle Fire HD.

viii. Do You Need an Anti-Virus?

It is always good to have anti-virus application installed on your device to prevent malware attack. Your tablet is prone to attack by viruses and malware every time you connect to the internet or download any third party software. You can search for antivirus applications in Amazon Apps for Android and choose one that meets your needs.

6.Browsing the Internet

i. Setting Up Email Accounts

The good news is that Kindle Fire HD includes email, contact and calendar applications which are compatible with popular services such as Gmail and Hotmail.

1. To add an email account, unlock and swipe down from the top of your screen.

2. Tap **Applications > Amazon Applications.**

3. Tap **Email, Contacts, Calendars,** and then hit **Add Account.**

4. Type your email account to finish set up.

5. To access your email account, first tap **Apps** on the home screen and then tap the email icon.

ii.   Connect with Social Media

Most Kindle Fire HD time users are really interested to know how they can use Facebook and other social media applications. You will be really pleased to know that your tablet has integrated support for popular applications such as Facebook and Twitter. And, you can download relevant applications from Apps for Android. These applications are specially optimized for Android OS and you can easily stay in touch with your friends.

iii. Privacy Control Options

Kindle Fire HD makes it really easy for you to restrict access to your tablet. You can set up **lock screen password** and **parental controls** to prevent unauthorized use of your device. If you feel you need to change settings under parental control, tap **More** in the menu that appears when you swipe down from the top of your screen.

iv.   Surfing the Web

Kindle Fire HD's web browser **'Silk'** is really easy to use. When your tablet is connected to a Wi-Fi network, you can tap 'Web' on your home screen and start browsing once the **Starter page** shows up. Your Starter page will also display sites that you visit frequently, popular pages trending on the web and other websites such as shopping and entertainment that may be of interest to you.

1. If you want to go to a web page, simply enter the address in the URL bar showing in your browser window and tap **Go**.

2. To return back to your main (Starter) page, first tap the **Menu icon** 📧 that appears at the bottom of your screen. You can then hit the Starter page option to go to your main page.

3. What makes Silk so popular is the fact that you can customize your viewing experience. Tap ✖ to enter full screen mode. You can exit full screen display by tapping the handle icon ▬ that appears at the bottom of your screen.

4. If you want to zoom in or out of a web page, all you have to do is 'pinch' the page you are currently viewing.

5. To download an item from the web, tap and hold the item. Tap **Save** using the message that appears on the screen. You can view the status of your download under notifications by pulling down the status bar. To access downloads, tap Menu 📧 on the bottom of the browser screen and then tap Downloads.

How Can You View Flash Content on Your Kindle Fire HD?

Your Kindle Fire HD does not support Flash content but you can make Flash –intensives websites work on your Silk browser. You can switch to mobile versions of the website to enjoy better browsing and website performance. If you want to switch to the mobile version, tap the Menu icon located at the bottom of your browser screen. Go to Settings > General > Requested Website View > Mobile to change your viewing preference.

Moreover, Adobe Flash Player is also not supported on Amazon tablets anymore. If you want to install Flash player on your Kindle Fire HD, first download a compatible web browser from an alternate source. You can then install Flash Player app that works with your new browser to run Flash supported content on your tablet.

v.   Bookmarking Favorites

You can easily bookmark a website while browsing the web on Kindle Fire HD. The **Add bookmark** button appears on the left side of the address bar. Tap the button and edit the name of the web page if you want. Tap **OK** to add the web page to your favorites.

vi.   Shopping with Kindle Fire HD

Kindle Fire HD is one of the best places to shop for books, movies, music, videos, applications and more. You are ready to start shopping once you've set up your **1 Click Payment account**. Just connect your tablet to a Wi-Fi network to select and purchase items from the online store. You can also connect to the Amazon.com website and purchase physical items using your Kindle Fire HD.

7.Reading Kindle Fire HD Style

i.   Kindle Books

You can tap **Books** on your home screen to view the collection you've downloaded from the Amazon cloud. If you want to read a particular book, tap on the item to start reading. Kindle Fire HD offers an amazing reading experience. You can tap the right side of your screen to go to the next page. Scroll to the left side and tap the screen to go to the previous page.

There is an interesting **Reading Toolbar** to enrich your viewing experience.

1. **Text Settings:** Helps you change font type, size and other settings.

2. **Go To:** Takes you to a specific location in your book. It can be a particular page or a chapter of your book .

3. **Notes:** Helps view the notes you mark. To add a note, press and hold on a word until a **contextual menu** appears on the screen. You can use the onscreen keyboard to type your note and then tap Save.

4. **X-Ray:** You can use X-Ray to learn more about characters and places in the book you are reading.

5. **Share:** Helps Share what you read on social media including Facebook and Twitter.

How Can You Transfer Books From Your Old Kindle or PC to Kindle Fire HD?

You can first download all content from your old Kindle to your computer. Once your files are stored on your computer's hard drive, you can connect the USB cable provided with Kindle Fire HD and transfer content with the help of guidelines mentioned on page 39 and 40 of this report.

ii. Quick Office

How Can You Create Documents on Kindle Fire HD?

Kindle Fire HD allows you to gain advantage in business and stay ahead in the competition. You can create and edit Microsoft Office Word documents, Excel spreadsheets and PowerPoint presentations right on your favorite tablet. **Quick Office Pro** is an exciting application you can download to stay connected with your documents. Moreover, this app also connects you to other useful services such as Google Docs, Dropbox and Evernote.

Can My Kindle Fire HD Display PowerPoint Presentations and PDF Documents?

Yes, your Kindle Fire HD comes preloaded with **basic Quick Office** which can be used to view MS Office documents, spreadsheets and presentations. You can also use basic Quick Office to view PDF files. However, you have to upgrade to Quick Office Pro to be able to create and edit documents.

iii.   Exploring Public Domain Library

The MOBI ebook or PDF files you download from the web are saved in your download folder. If you want to see the free eBooks you've downloaded in your books folder, you need to download a compatible File Manager application. Once file manager app is installed, you can use it to transfer your free eBooks to the relevant folder.

iv.   Manage Your Kindle Books

Kindle Fire HD helps you keep track of your reading habits. A progress bar indicates how much of the book you have read. You can easily go to the table of contents, cover design or the furthest page using the Menu icon. Your Kindle Fire HD also features the *New Oxford American Dictionary*. All you have to do is tap and highlight the word you want to be defined.

8.Kindle 3G and Kindle Fire HD – What's the Difference?

Feature	Kindle Paperwhite 3G	Kindle Fire HD	Kindle touch 3G
Screen size	6 inches	7 inches or 8.9 inches	6 inches
Screen resolution	768x1024	1280x800	600X800
E-ink electronic paper	Yes	No	Yes
Screen type	Paperwhite Built-in light	IPS (In-Plane Switching technology)	eInk pearl
Wireless technology	Wi-Fi, 3G	Wi-Fi	Wi-Fi, 3G
Wi-Fi	Enabled	Enabled Dual band	Enabled
Bluetooth®	Not Available	Enabled	Not Available
HDMI port	Not Available	Available	Not Available
Internal memory storage	2 GB	16 GB to 32 GB	4 GB
Front camera	No	Yes	No
Rear camera	No	No	No

9.Root Kindle Fire HD – Just Like That

Are you one of the Android enthusiasts looking for ways to root your Kindle Fire HD? "Rooting" basically allows you to run applications that can easily make changes to your systems data and resources. Here are some steps you can follow to root your Kindle Fire HD.

1. Enable ADB (Android Debug Bridge) for your platform (Windows, Mac or Linux) from *Settings > Security*.

2. Download *Kindle_Fire_HD_ADB_Drivers.zip* from http://rootzwiki.com. Open the zip file and extract the contents. Make sure you launch the executable file within the zip folder.

3. Download *Superuser-3.1.3-arm-signed.zip* from http://rootzwiki.com. You will find a *system* folder and within that, locate *Superuser.apk* and an *su* file.

4. Copy and paste both Superuser.apk and su to the **PLATFORM-TOOLS** folder. You should paste both the files in the same directory you have installed Android SDK.

5. Connect your tablet to the computer and launch a terminal program. Go to *platform-tools* folder and the same directory where you've installed Android SDK.

6. Enter the following commands one at a time in the same order. Your device should be rooted if you followed the steps correctly.

adb shell

rm -r /data/local/tmp

ln -s /data/ /data/local/tmp

exit

adb reboot

```
adb shell

echo 'ro.kernel.qemu=1' > /data/local.prop

exit


adb reboot


adb shell mount -o remount,rw /system

adb push su /system/xbin/su

adb shell

chown 0.0 /system/xbin/su

chmod 06755 /system/xbin/su

rm /data/local.prop

exit


adb reboot


adb install Superuser.apk
```

10. Conclusion

At the end of this guide, you will be familiar with the amazing and exciting features of your tablet – Kindle Fire HD. You now know ways to use your Kindle and how you can get the most of your favorite gadget. This guide has put lots of best 'up to date' information in one place so that you can stay connected with your device. You surely must have found this guide useful and using Kindle Fire HD is not really a tough task now!

Thanks for staying together and hopefully you can now unleash the powerful features your tablet offers.

Also Check Out My other Book

Windows 8: Discover The Secret To

Unleash The Power Of Windows 8!

www.ingramcontent.com/pod-product-compliance
Lightning Source LLC
Chambersburg PA
CBHW050936060326

40689CB00040B/596